If Scars Could Speak

The Gospel according to my pain

By

Sunday Jones

www.ingramcontent.com/pod-product-compliance
Lightning Source LLC
Chambersburg PA
CBHW070903130626
46555CB00001B/10

www.sundayjoneswrites.com

ISBN: [9798999462824]

Cover design by Sunday Jones

Printed in the United States

Dedication:

To the little girl who survived what should've broken her.

To the grown woman who found her voice inside the silence.

To every soul that has been scarred, overlooked, forgotten, or betrayed—

this book is for you.

For your healing. For your truth. For your power.

To my ancestors, your whispers live in my walk.

To God, your light lives in my words.

And to every woman who's ever wept behind closed doors, this gospel is yours too.

With all my scars, I offer you my truth.

– Sunday Jones

I Honor

Marty "MartyPix" Frierson my brother that saved me and raised me I love you. Terrell " My Twin" Wilkinson rocking since day I until the wheels fall off and beyond. Rodney "DublR" Reid thanks for showing me a different kind of love. Adam Wilkinson for always being their. Emory "DJ EJ Highmoney" Sheffield my favorite DJ & friend I got you like you got name always. Antione "Murda" Wright when I was sick you cared for me like a brother protected me when needed and ill always be your lil sis. Lil Marty Frierson I got them no worries I miss you, Renita D. Starr my bestie you saved my life & gave me 5 beautiful god children. Mercedes Moultrie my go to sister cousin more like sisters than cousins, Sarah Bakas my friend to the end held me during my worst moments. Tanya "Tiny" Warner, Denise "ShawnDee" Sanders, my sisters and business partners I love y'all.

BeBe Frierson my sister your the best. Nadine Frierson the mom that gave me what I needed when mine was unable. Briggitte "Lil Mama" Harper always my lil momma big sister thank you for the lessons. Hope "Melo" Rugley my friend my family my business partner I love you. Norma "Diamond" Jones for all the love yo showed me while you were here. Emma Starr thank you for the well you allowed me to drink from. Aretha "Ree" Wilkinson my rider I miss you so much. Auntie Loyce Wilkinson my prayer warrior my reassurance in love & God. ,Tassili Maat for believing in me, Ya'ah Ya'ah Santana for loving me so. Carolyn Wilkinson for always loving me purely. My TiTi for keeping us. If your name isn't here its not because I forgot you. I just can't fit everyone.

A LETTER TO MYSELF

Dear Sunday,

I'm proud of you.

I don't think I've said that enough—
not to the girl you were,
not to the woman you became,
and not to the soul who kept fighting
even when everything around you
said give up.

You carried burdens
that weren't yours to hold.

You loved people

who didn't know how to love you back.

You survived storms

that were designed to break you

but instead built you.

You have walked through fire

without losing your softness.

You have rebuilt yourself

from pieces no one else saw.

You have risen

again and again—

not because life made it easy,

but because purpose

wouldn't let you quit.

I want you to know:

You deserved love

even when you didn't receive it.

You deserved protection

even when no one covered you.

You deserved rest

even when the world demanded strength.

And now—

you deserve joy without explanation,

peace without permission,

healing without apology.

Thank you for choosing yourself.

Thank you for not letting the world

harden your heart.

Thank you for believing

there was more to your life

than the pain you inherited.

I love the woman you are becoming.

I honor the girl who got you here.

And I promise

to keep pouring into you

the way no one ever poured into her.

With grace, truth, gratitude,

and all the softness you earned,

— Sunday BSSW Jones

Ella J. Wilkinson-Shipp (Mother), McAvoy
"Daddy Mac" Shipp, (Me) Sunday BSSW-
Jones

" One of my most favorite memories with the man I thought was my dad until I was 7 " before she went to prison, while he was still there. They loved me, but made big mistakes since they both went to prison for a long time.

Dear Reader,

Thank you for being here.

Thank you for opening these pages,

for choosing to face truth with me,

for walking into a body of work

that was born from pain,

shaped by survival,

and reborn through healing.

This book is not just poetry—

it is memory,

testimony,

and transformation

stitched together with honesty.

I don't know what brought you here—

a heartbreak you're still holding,

a childhood wound you've never named,

a loss you're learning to live with,

or simply the desire

to feel less alone.

But I do know this:

You were meant to read this.

Every word in this book

was written with a heartbeat behind it—

mine,

and now,

yours.

As you move through these pages,

I pray you recognize yourself

in the rising.

I pray something awakens in you—

a truth you forgot,

a strength you buried,

a softness you thought you lost.

Take your time here.

Pause when a line grips you.

Cry when something breaks open.

Breathe when a piece hits too close.

Highlight your healing

as it unfolds.

And when you close this book,

I hope you leave lighter

than you came.

With love, truth, and grace,

— Sunday Jones

Table of Contents

BONUS SECTION

PART I

THE PAIN THAT SHAPED ME

I: BEFORE THE STREETS

Before the streets knew my name,

before I ever learned to armor up in hardness

and hustle,

I was just a little girl

sitting in the chaos of grown folks' decisions.

I was raised in a house where the walls had

memories

they never got to forget.

Where voices were louder than prayers,

and bruises showed up faster than hugs.

My mama went away when I was five.

Not on vacation.

Not to a new job.

But to a place where metal doors locked behind you

and time passed different.

That's when I learned what silence sounded like

when it didn't mean peace.

That's when the streets started whispering to me

—

not with promises,

but with presence.

Because the love I craved wasn't home.

And when nobody came to rescue me,

I rescued myself.

Piece by piece,

I hardened.

I toughened.

I became what I thought I had to become

to survive the heat around me.

And yet,

deep inside that survival suit,

was a girl still looking for softness,

for safety,

for someone to say:

"You shouldn't have had to grow up like that."

Before the streets,

I was somebody's daughter.

Somebody's baby girl.

Before the bruises,

before the molestors,

before the betrayal and blame,

I was just a child

trying to make sense of it all.

So if you ever wonder why I walk like I've seen
too much—

it's because I have.

Not on the streets.

But before them.

POEM 2: IF SCARS COULD SPEAK

If scars could speak,

mine would hum gospel hymns in broken

harmony,

a choir of closed wounds singing survival songs

in off-key hallelujahs.

They'd whisper the names of every night I almost

didn't make it,

every silent scream tucked into the corner of my

smile,

every prayer I didn't know I was praying

when I kept showing up.

They'd speak in tongues only pain understands
—

like, the language of looking strong

while bleeding inside your ribcage,

or smiling when your whole soul is sobbing.

If scars could speak,

they'd remind me I am both battlefield and healer,

both the war and the peace that followed,

a mosaic made of moments that didn't break me.

They'd testify.

They'd say:

"She survived herself.

She buried her old life and planted herself instead."

They'd say:

"She chose to bloom anyway."

Because these scars don't shame me—

they name me.

They crown me.

They remind me I am a walking redemption song.

POEM 3: THE GOSPEL TO MY PAIN

This ain't your Sunday sermon

but the gospel still got weight.

It's the gospel according to my pain—

unedited, unchurchified,

still drenched in grace.

It's the cracked-open Bible I became,

pages torn by trauma,

scriptures rewritten in survival,

verses baptized in my tears

and redeemed in my becoming.

This gospel starts at rock bottom,

where my voice broke

and my knees met concrete,

where the only "amen" I knew

was my own breath—still here.

I laid hands on myself when nobody else would.

I called healing down like rain

and watched it soften even the hardest parts of

me.

I stopped waiting for a pulpit

and became my own preacher.

This gospel don't quote Paul—

it quotes pain,

quotes nights I didn't think I'd wake up,

quotes healing that happened in silence.

And baby, that's holy too.

POEM 4: WHEN HE HAD THAT BABY

When he had that baby

outside of me,

outside of us,

outside of all the promises he fed me

like stale bread I still tried to chew,

I choked on my silence.

That baby wasn't mine—

but the heartbreak was.

It rocked me, gutted me,

made me question if I ever existed

or was I just a womb he bypassed

on his way to someone else's forever.

I checked out.

Emotionally packed my bags

and started unpacking my worth

in a place where he couldn't reach it.

I stopped calling,

stopped performing love in a play

I didn't audition for.

Started checking in with myself

like a mother would her own child—

soft, gentle,

apologizing for every time I ignored the signs.

When he had that baby,

I gave birth too—

to the woman I had buried

beneath excuses and "maybe he'll change."

I held her.

I raised her.

I became her again.

POEM 5: THE SILENCE BETWEEN SCREAMS

Some pain don't holler—

it hums.

It sits in the throat

like an unspoken truth

too heavy to carry,

too dangerous to drop.

It's the pause between sobs,

the calm before the collapse,

the stare into nothing

that says everything.

You ever scream so loud inside

that nobody hears you outside?

That's where I lived—

in the silence between screams.

I mastered the art of smiling through storms,

laughing while leaking,

performing okay

like it paid the bills.

But silence—

that silence?

She ain't passive.

She's a killer.

So I learned to name it.

To speak the ache.

To scream when I needed to

and whisper when I didn't.

Now I live out loud.

Now my healing makes noise.

POEM 6: BAGGAGE CLAIM

They told me time heals all wounds—

but never told me healing comes with carry-ons.

Luggage full of "I forgave him"

next to a tote bag of triggers.

I unpack slowly now.

Piece by piece.

Unfolding the shame

I packed so neatly

behind strength.

There's a suitcase labeled

"childhood,"

another marked

"the way mama loved me."

Inside are clothes that never fit

and stories that still do.

But I no longer let my baggage

board flights I'm not on.

I no longer apologize

for the weight I carry

or the care I take in checking it.

Healing ain't about pretending you're empty.

It's knowing what you carry

and choosing to sort through it.

One bag at a time.

POEM 7: THE SCARS ON THE INSIDE

Not all wounds wear red.

Some dress in silence,

camouflaged behind laughter,

veiled in lipstick and productivity.

They don't scab—

they shadow.

Don't bleed—

they burden.

They live in the pauses

between "I'm fine" and "I wish someone would

ask again."

In the tension of holding it together

while feeling like dust on the inside.

But I see them—

the scars that don't show.

I name them.

I honor them.

I know their stories.

Because some healing

ain't about what you show—

it's about what you survive quietly,

what you carry gracefully,

what you turn into wisdom.

And those?

Those scars are sacred too.

POEM 8: I'M WHAT MOST CALL AN EMPATH

I'm what most call an empath—

but really, I'm a spiritual sensor

in a world that runs off static.

I can feel storms

before the clouds even gather,

sense tension

in a room dressed in smiles,

taste lies

even when they wear sugar.

I know what you're not saying—

not because I'm nosy,

but because I was trained in silence.

My survival depended on noticing

what others ignored.

I used to think it was a burden—

to feel so deeply,

to cry over things that hadn't happened yet,

to hurt for people

who'd already moved on.

But now I know

it's a gift.

And like all gifts—

it must be protected.

I no longer absorb everything.

I discern.

I filter.

I release.

I'm not a sponge for sorrow.

I'm a vessel for light.

And that light

has boundaries now.

PART II

BETRAYAL, BREAKDOWNS & BECOMINGS

POEM 9: UNLEARNING SURVIVAL

I didn't know I was still in fight mode

until peace felt foreign.

I didn't know I was flinching

at every kindness

until someone offered me love

and I mistook it for a setup.

See, survival taught me

how to read the room,

how to laugh in chaos,

how to build a fortress from silence.

But survival is not the same as living.

It doesn't teach you softness—

only how to stay alert.

I had to unlearn

the twitch in my spirit

that said, "Be ready to run."

Had to rewire

the belief that rest meant weakness.

I no longer crown my scars

as trophies of who hurt me.

I honor them

as proof of how far I've come.

I don't owe survival my loyalty.

I owe healing my attention.

And now,

I choose softness

without apology.

POEM 10: THE WOMAN I'VE BECOME IS WATCHING

She stands behind me

like a shadow made of light—

the woman I'm becoming.

She watches my choices

and whispers,

"Don't forget who you're becoming for."

She doesn't beg for approval.

She doesn't shrink to survive.

She walks in the room

with purpose braided in her spine

and softness sewn in her voice.

She's the version of me

that no longer explains her boundaries

or breaks herself to stay palatable.

She's healed,

but not quiet.

Whole,

but not hard.

And every time I want to fall back

into patterns that kept me small,

she raises one eyebrow like,

"Oh... we still doing that?"

She is my reminder

that I have already outgrown

what I once accepted.

And she's waiting

on the other side of my choices.

So I move with her in mind.

Because the woman I've become

is watching.

POEM 11 : THE DAY I FINALLY FORGAVE MYSELF

The day I finally forgave myself,

I didn't light a candle

or whisper a fancy affirmation.

I didn't sit cross-legged in meditation

or write a letter to my younger self.

I simply exhaled.

A long, trembling breath

that carried years of shame on its back—

shame I never deserved,

but wore like it was tailored for me.

I forgave myself

for the men I loved who broke me,

for the nights I stayed when I should've run,

for the moments I abandoned my own intuition

just to feel chosen.

I forgave myself

for the little girl in me

who thought she had to earn softness.

For the woman in me

who thought survival required silence.

I forgave myself

for being human—

for bleeding,

for breaking,

for healing slower than I wanted to.

And when I did,

I felt something shift.

Like a door inside me creaked open

and light crawled in on its hands and knees.

Forgiving myself

wasn't letting myself off the hook—

it was letting myself off the cross.

POEM 12 : ALMOST LOST THE LOVE I DESERVE

I prayed for a love that saw me.

And when it finally came—

gentle, patient, honest—

I damn near ran from it.

Not because it wasn't real,

but because real scared me.

I carried so many old wounds

I kept bleeding on someone

who wasn't holding the knife.

I flinched at kindness.

Side-eyed consistency.

Prepared for abandonment

before it even arrived.

Trauma had trained me

to hear footsteps leaving

even when no one moved.

But he stayed.

Not to rescue me—

to remind me

that love doesn't always hurt.

Still, I almost lost it.

Not because he was wrong...

but because I wasn't healed.

I learned the hard way:

you can ask God for a blessing

and still sabotage it

when you haven't released

the ghosts you sleep beside.

I'm grateful I woke up in time—

grateful I learned that love

isn't something you brace for.

It's something you step into

with both hands open.

POEM 13 : HE KISSED ME THROUGH MY GRIEF

I was breaking quietly.

Held together by thin threads

of strength I didn't recognize anymore.

Grief sat on my chest

like a storm that forgot to move on—

heavy, stubborn,

flooding everything in silence.

And then he showed up.

Not to save me.

Not to fix what death had undone.

But to sit with me

in the ache.

He held space

the way some men hold pride—

tight, protective, unshaking.

When he kissed me,

it wasn't passion.

It was presence.

A soft reminder

that even in your darkest hour,

you are still held.

He didn't rush my tears.

Didn't hush my trembling.

Didn't fear the weight

of what I was carrying.

He just kissed me

slow, grounding,

like he was trying to stitch

my spirit back together

one breath at a time.

And for the first time in months,

I felt something

other than pain.

POEM 14 : PEACE AIN'T PASSIVE- IT'S A FIGHT

People talk about peace

like it's a pillow—

soft, fluffy, effortless.

But peace is work.

Peace is warfare.

Peace is choosing your sanity

over your story,

your future

over your familiar.

Peace requires swinging sometimes—

not at people,

but at old patterns

trying to drag you back

into versions of yourself

you outgrew.

Peace is saying "no"

even when your voice shakes.

Cutting ties

even when your heart lingers.

Walking away

even when your knees wobble.

Peace is a decision—

and baby, it ain't passive.

It's removing yourself

from the rooms

where your spirit suffocates.

It's blocking numbers

God been told you to block.

It's choosing quiet

over chaos

even when chaos is more exciting.

Peace ain't soft.

It's sacred.

And every time you protect it,

you win a battle

your younger self prayed you'd survive.

POEM 15 : FORGIVENESS AIN'T EASY, BUT NECESSARY

Forgiveness is a slow walk—

not a lightning strike.

It's peeling back layers

of resentment,

disappointment,

betrayals that still echo

in your ribs.

Forgiveness is not forgetting—

it's remembering without reopening the wound.

It's understanding you can let go

without letting someone back in.

I had to learn

that forgiving them

wasn't about them.

It was about freeing myself

from the weight of carrying

what wasn't mine to hold.

Forgiving myself

was even harder.

Because self-blame

sticks like wet clothes,

heavy and cold

against the skin.

But necessary doesn't mean easy—

it just means worth it.

Forgiveness isn't the door.

It's the key.

The one that unlocks

your next version of peace.

POEM 16 : THE MIRROR DOESN'T LIE

The mirror doesn't lie—

even when I wish it would.

It shows the truth

behind my practiced smile,

the exhaustion sitting heavy

beneath my eyelids,

the softness I've earned

and the pain I've survived

etched in the curves of my face.

I used to be afraid

to look too long—

afraid I'd see the woman

who stayed too long,

loved too hard,

carried too much.

But the mirror also showed me

the woman who rose anyway—

the warrior with trembling knees,

the healer with shattered hands,

the survivor who kept choosing life

when life didn't choose her back.

Now, when I stand before it,

I don't search for perfection.

I look for proof.

Proof that I'm still here.
Proof that I've grown.
Proof that the woman staring back at me
is no longer begging to be understood—
she understands herself.

And that truth
is more beautiful
than flawless skin
or untangled pasts.

The mirror doesn't lie.
But finally, neither do I.

POEM 17 : GOSPEL ACCORDING TO THE HOOD

The hood taught me sermons

no preacher ever preached.

Lessons wrapped in streetlights,

echoed in sirens,

written in the eyes of kids

who grew up too fast

and trusted too few.

The gospel according to the hood says:

Protect your heart.

Move with intention.

Never mistake noise for power.

And don't you ever forget

who you were before the world tried you.

It taught me

loyalty matters,

but loyalty to yourself

matters more.

It taught me

some family ain't blood—

it's bond,

it's survival,

it's who held you down

when your world was coming apart.

It taught me

to read people

better than books,

to hear danger in footsteps,

to sense betrayal

before the words left their mouth.

But the hood also taught me love—

the kind that shows up

with folded arms and open hands,

the kind that feeds you

when your soul is starving,

the kind that says,

"You good?"

and means it.

The gospel according to the hood

didn't save my life—

it shaped it.

And I thank God

for every chapter.

POEM 18 : DIVINE ACCOUNTABILITY

Some people call it intuition—

I call it divine accountability.

That moment when Source taps you

on the back of your spirit

and whispers,

"You know better."

Accountability ain't punishment—

it's protection.

It's wisdom showing up

before the wound.

It's the warning you feel

before the fall you don't need.

For years, I ignored the signs—

the tightening in my chest,

the heaviness in my gut,

the ancestors tugging on my sleeve saying,

"Baby, that's not your path."

But growth taught me this:

The Most High will never force your healing,

but will always reveal your truth.

Divine accountability

is when God shows you yourself—

not to shame you,

but to shape you.

It asks:

Are you done repeating cycles?

Are you finished abandoning yourself?

Are you finally ready

to step into the woman

your pain prepared you to become?

This ain't discipline.

This is destiny.

And I answer now

with my whole chest:

"Yes."

POEM 19 : KNOW YOUR WORTH

You are not a bargain-bin blessing,

not a discount destiny,

not a clearance-rack creation

marked down for the convenience

of people who never learned

how to value anything.

Stop letting people handle you

with unwashed hands

and unhealed hearts.

Stop shrinking so others

can feel tall in your presence.

Stop accepting crumbs

when you were baked

to be a feast.

Know your worth—

and then add tax.

Know your power—

and then multiply it.

Know your beauty—

the kind that doesn't fade

when the lights go off

or the world goes quiet.

You are the prayer

somebody whispered

in their darkest hour.

You are the breath

somebody needed

to keep going.

And when love comes knocking,

if it ain't wearing respect,

if it ain't carrying peace,

if it ain't dressed in consistency—

don't you dare open the door.

You are becoming.

And that alone

is holy ground.

POEM 20 : SOFT GIRL ERA (BEFORE LOVE)

Before love found me,

I was a fortress—

brick layered on brick,

guarded gate,

no entry,

no exceptions.

Softness felt like a luxury

I couldn't afford.

Gentleness felt like a risk

I didn't trust myself to take.

I had been hardened

by disappointments,

sharpened by survival,

shaped by wounds

that didn't heal

as fast as people thought.

I wore strength

like a shield

and silence

like armor.

But even then—

beneath the metal,

beneath the grit,

beneath the girl who always found a way—

there lived a softness

I never stopped craving.

A softness waiting

for a safe place to land.

A softness waiting

to breathe again.

A softness waiting

for a love

that wouldn't mistake it

for weakness.

This was me

before love:

strong,

tired,

hopeful,

guarded—

and ready

even when I didn't know it.

POEM 21 : SOFT GIRL ERA (AFTER LOVE)

After love found me,

I felt myself unclench.

My shoulders softened.

My jaw released its grip

on years of silent battles.

I breathed—

not to survive,

but to receive.

I didn't know softness

could feel like safety.

I didn't know love

could move slow,

steady,

and still feel certain.

With him,

my guard didn't fall—

it dissolved.

Piece by piece,

without force,

without fear.

He didn't demand my softness;

he created space for it.

He didn't rush my healing;

he honored it.

And the girl inside me—

the one who had been holding her breath—

finally exhaled.

This era isn't about a man—

it's about me.

Me choosing tenderness

over toughness,

receiving instead of resisting,

letting my feminine rest

instead of roar.

This era is where

my heart feels heard,

my spirit feels held,

and my softness

finally feels safe.

POEM 22 : THIS LOVE WAS DIFFERENT

This love didn't show up loud—

it arrived like morning light,

quiet but undeniable.

It didn't demand attention.

It earned it.

It didn't promise forever.

It offered presence.

This love felt like water—

gentle enough to soothe me,

strong enough to hold me,

wise enough to flow around

the jagged edges

of the places I was still healing.

He didn't love me

for who he wanted me to be;

he loved me

for who I already was.

My scars didn't scare him.

My silence didn't confuse him.

My strength didn't threaten him.

He saw me—

the me behind the bravado,

the me beneath the armor,

the me who still prayed

for the kind of love

that didn't feel like a gamble.

And with him,

I learned something new:

Love isn't supposed to hurt.

Love isn't a battlefield.

Love isn't a test.

This love

was different.

And so was I.

POEM 23 : GOD IM LISTENING

I used to pray through clenched teeth,

only half-believing

God heard me through the noise

of my own doubt.

I'd ask for signs

and then argue with them.

Ask for guidance

and then choose chaos.

Ask for peace

and then run straight back

to my storms.

But life has a way

of humbling you—

of sitting you down

in the middle of your mess

and saying,

"Now... are you ready to listen?"

And I was.

When the walls caved in,

when the lies hit harder,

when the heartbreak finally cracked

the last place I was hiding—

I whispered,

"Okay, God.

I'm listening now."

And God spoke—

not in thunder,

not in fire,

but in clarity.

Leave that.

Choose you.

Walk here.

Not there.

Rest now.

Rise later.

And for the first time,

I trusted the stillness.

Trusted the pull.

Trusted the God in me

that had been nudging all along.

Now my life is quieter—

not empty,

just aligned.

"God, I'm listening now."

And every day,

I hear more.

POEM 24 : THE WOMAN WHO RAISED HERSELF

I didn't grow up

with hands that held me gently

or voices that affirmed me.

I didn't grow up

with guidance, protection,

or a blueprint for love.

So I became the woman

who raised herself.

I learned to mend my own wounds,

bandage my own heart,

clean up the messes

of people who taught me

more about pain

than nurturing.

I taught myself

how to stand tall,

how to walk away,

how to stay soft

in a world that tried

to harden every inch of me.

I mothered the parts of me

that never got mothered.

Fed my soul compassion

when my childhood fed me chaos.

Held my own hand

through storms

no child should've weathered.

And now,

when I look in the mirror,

I don't just see a woman.

I see a survivor

who became her own sanctuary.

The woman who raised herself

deserves everything blooming in her life now—

because she planted every seed

with broken fingers and still made a garden.

POEM 25 : LESSONS FROM THE STORM

The storm didn't come to destroy me—

it came to teach.

It taught me

who I was

when everything fell apart.

It taught me

who had my back

when the thunder got loud.

It taught me

what I needed to release

and what I needed to reclaim.

Storms reveal truths

sunlight hides.

They show you

which relationships were rooted

and which were weeds.

Which fears were lies

and which warnings were wisdom.

Which parts of you

were built on faith

and which on fear.

I learned

I am stronger than my past,

softer than my pain,

and wiser than the mistakes

I once thought defined me.

I learned

that breaking

isn't the end—

it's the clearing.

And every storm

that tried to drown me

ended up washing me clean.

Learning to Love yourself, trust yourself, and be yourself is the most important lesson of all. Keep your cup full. Its a daily work, its not overnight or something you can stop doing. Stay consistent on loving yourself.

PART III

THE BECOMING

POEM 26 : WHAT I THOUGHT WAS LOVE

What I thought was love

was really survival dressed up

in romance language.

It was me confusing attachment

with devotion,

chaos with chemistry,

consistency with control.

It was me mistaking butterflies

for anxiety,

apologies

for accountability,

and pain

for passion.

I called it love

because I didn't know

what love felt like

without bruises—

emotional or otherwise.

I thought love

was supposed to hurt a little,

supposed to break you open,

supposed to make you lose pieces

of yourself

just to keep someone whole.

But what I thought was love

was really fear—

fear of being alone,

fear of starting over,

fear of not being enough

for anyone else.

Now I know better.

Now I know

love doesn't take your breath—

it teaches you how to breathe.

Love doesn't drain you—

it pours into you.

Love doesn't demand sacrifice—

it inspires reciprocity.

What I thought was love

wasn't love at all.

Just a lesson

wearing a mask

I was finally brave enough

to remove.

POEM 27 : THE GIRL I BURIED TO SURVIVE

There was a girl inside me—

bright, soft, curious,

full of wonder and open hands—

and I buried her.

Not because I wanted to,

but because the world insisted

she was too vulnerable

to survive.

So I wrapped her

in silence.

Covered her

in armor.

Protected her

with attitude

and sharpened edges.

She watched from underneath

as I toughened up,

as I learned to hide my tenderness

behind humor,

my hurt

behind ambition,

my fear

behind resilience.

But she never left.

She stayed

waiting for a time

when safety meant something real,

when love wasn't a gamble,

when I stopped mistaking strength

for suppression.

And when I finally healed enough

to hear her—

really hear her—

she whispered:

"I never needed you to bury me.

I needed you to fight for me."

So now,

I make room for her.

I let her laugh louder,

dream bigger,

cry softer.

I am becoming the woman

who rescues

the girl I once abandoned.

POEM 28 : NOW I RISE LIKE THIS

I used to rise

because I had no choice.

Because staying down

meant drowning

in the same waters

I learned to swim through.

But now—

now I rise differently.

Not from fear,

but from faith.

Not from pressure,

but from purpose.

Not because life pushed me—

but because God pulled me.

I rise

with intention.

With softness.

With clarity.

With boundaries

that don't apologize.

I rise

knowing what I carry,

knowing what I release,

knowing who I am

and who I refuse to be again.

I rise

for the women who look to me,

for the girls who come after me,

for the ancestors who guide me,

and for the version of me

who almost didn't survive

to see this day.

I rise

like a prayer answered.

Like a promise kept.

Like healing learned

the hard way.

I rise

because I was born to—

and because staying down

was never my destiny.

POEM 29 : TO THE MEN WHO PROTECT US

To the men who protect us—

not with fists or fear,

but with presence,

patience,

and truth:

We see you.

To the brothers, cousins, fathers,

lovers, friends, and souls

who show up

with steady hands

and listening hearts—

we honor you.

To the men who say,

"I got you,"

and mean it.

To the men who stand

between us and the world

when the world gets loud—

this poem is your flowers.

You are the quiet warriors,

the soft shoulders,

the protectors who don't perform it

for applause.

You pour into us

without draining yourself.

You lead

without controlling.

You love

without harming.

And for every moment

you held space for our breaking

without flinching,

for every time

you reinforced our strength

without silencing our softness—

thank you.

May you always be covered,

always be lifted,

always be poured into

the way you pour into us.

This world is better

because you carry your purpose

with dignity.

POEM 30 : LETTER TO MY INNER CHILD

Dear little me—

I'm sorry.

Not for what you went through,

because none of it was your fault,

but for all the years

I didn't know how to protect you.

I'm sorry I silenced your tears

to keep the peace.

Sorry I hid your softness

to survive the chaos.

Sorry I told you

you were too sensitive,

too needy,

too much

for people who weren't enough.

But look at you now—

still here,

still beating,

still believing in love

though it wasn't always kind to you.

I want you to know this:

You are safe with me now.

I listen to you.

I fight for you.

I make choices

that honor the girl you were

and the woman you became.

You don't have to be brave anymore.

Not for them.

Not for me.

Not for the world.

You just have to be loved.

And baby,

you are.

With my whole healed heart,

I promise you this:

I will never abandon you again.

POEM 31 : TO THE WOMAN WHO'S STILL IN IT

To the woman who's still in it—

still loving him,

still hurting,

still trying to leave

while trying to stay,

still praying for clarity

but fearing the answer...

I see you.

You're not weak.

You're not foolish.

You're not blind.

You're human.

You're hopeful.

You're healing

in the middle of the storm

that's been disguised as love.

You're doing your best

with the tools you were given

in a world that taught you

to prioritize others

and survive yourself.

Let me tell you this gently:

You deserve a love

that doesn't make you question

your value.

You deserve a peace

that doesn't break

when the door closes.

You deserve a safety

that doesn't shake

with someone else's mood.

You deserve

what you've been trying

to give away.

And whenever you're ready—

not rushed,

not shamed,

not pushed—

but ready...

Your freedom will meet you

right where you are.

Until then,

be kind to yourself.

You're not behind.

You're not lost.

You're becoming.

POEM 32 : WHEN I FINALLY FELT SAFE

It didn't happen all at once.

Safety came in layers—

slow, gentle,

like the thaw after winter.

It was the way he said my name

without raising his voice.

The way he waited for me

to finish my thoughts

instead of talking over my fear.

The way he didn't flinch

when my trauma showed up

uninvited.

Safety was not a moment—

it was a collection of moments.

Tiny pieces of peace

I gathered over time

until one day,

my body realized

it didn't need to brace anymore.

I felt safe

when my nervous system

stopped preparing for the worst.

When silence didn't feel like punishment.

When affection didn't feel like a setup.

When I stopped rehearsing

my exit strategy.

I didn't know safety

could feel like softness.

I didn't know security

could feel like rest.

But when I finally felt safe—

truly safe—

I understood this:

Love is not loud.

Love is steady.

Love is shelter.

And my spirit

finally walked inside.

POEM 33 : HEALING DON'T MEAN YOU FORGET

People think healing

means the memories fade,

the heartbreak erases,

the scars soften

until they disappear.

But healing

ain't divine amnesia.

Healing means

you remember—

you just don't relive.

You recall—

but you don't return.

You reflect—

but you don't reopen.

Healing means

you can tell the story

without tasting blood.

Means you can see their face

without losing yourself.

Means your body

no longer mistakes

familiar pain

for current danger.

Healing don't mean you forget.

It means the past

no longer interrupts

your present.

It means the lesson

outgrew the wound.

It means you can finally say:

"This happened to me,

but it isn't me."

Healing is not forgetting—

it's remembering

without breaking.

POEM 34 : GRIEF STILL VISITS ME SOMETIME

Grief doesn't knock.

It walks in like it still lives here—

opens my fridge,

sits on my couch,

puts its feet up

like it never left.

And sometimes,

I let it.

I let myself remember

the warmth of who I lost,

the echo of their laughter,

the shape of their absence

in rooms that used to hold them.

Grief still visits me sometimes—

on quiet mornings,

in crowded spaces,

in songs I wasn't ready to hear,

in moments when joy

feels like betrayal.

But I don't fight it anymore.

I learned

that grief doesn't come to reopen wounds—

it comes to honor love.

It's the shadow of a bond

too deep to die

just because a heartbeat stopped.

So when grief visits,

I breathe.

I let it stay

for a moment—

not forever.

I thank it

for reminding me of love

big enough to miss.

And then,

when it's ready,

it leaves—

quietly,

like a guest

who knows

they'll always have a key.

POEM 35 : GOD MET ME IN MY CHAOS

I didn't find God

in a church pew

or a perfect moment

of clarity.

God met me

in the middle of my chaos.

In the nights

when my tears soaked the pillow

and my prayers had no words.

In the mornings

when I dragged my spirit

into the sunlight

hoping it would warm

what life had frozen.

God met me

when I couldn't pretend anymore.

When my strength snapped.

When my pride cracked.

When my survival mode

finally malfunctioned.

God was there

in every breakdown

that felt like failure

but was really a doorway.

In every silence

that felt like abandonment

but was really preparation.

I didn't rise

because I was strong.

I rose

because God lifted me.

In the chaos,

in the noise,

in the heartbreak,

in the confusion—

God was not absent.

God was working.

And now I know

the truth:

Sometimes the storm

is not meant to break you—

it's meant to introduce you

to the God

that carries you through it.

POEM 36 : THE WOMAN I AM TODAY

The woman I am today

wasn't built in calm waters.

She was shaped

in the deep end—

where breath runs thin,

where faith is tested,

where strength isn't a choice

but a lifeline.

The woman I am today

walked through fire

without knowing if she'd make it out.

And when she did,

she didn't come out the same—

she came out glowing.

She speaks softer now,

not because she's weak,

but because she's learned

that peace doesn't shout.

She loves differently now,

not from emptiness

or fear of loneliness,

but from fullness—

from a healed heart

that pours with intention.

The woman I am today

forgives faster,

trusts slower,

loves deeper,

and leaves sooner

when her spirit says,

"This ain't it."

She is the evidence

that broken crayons still color,

shattered pieces still shine,

and wounded women

still rise.

And baby—

she is just getting started.

POEM 37 : A DIFFERENT KIND OF HOLY

I used to think holiness

lived only in churches—

in stained glass windows,

in choir robes,

in hands lifted high

toward heaven.

But I found a different kind of holy

in the places life bruised me.

Holy was the moment

I chose myself

after choosing everyone else

nearly killed me.

Holy was the night

I cried so hard

I met God in my own breathing.

Holy was the boundary

I finally set

with people I used to break for.

Holy was the peace

that came after the leaving,

after the breaking,

after the truth

tore my world apart

so I could rebuild it right.

My healing is holy.

My growth is holy.

My clarity is holy.

My survival—

that's holy too.

I am sacred

because I lived.

I am divine

because I rose.

This is a different kind of holy—

one that lives in me,

moves through me,

and guides me

every time I forget

who I truly am.

POEM 38 : BECOMING SUNDAY

Before I became Sunday,

I was a girl named Survival.

I woke up fighting,

went to bed fighting,

loved while fighting,

lived while fighting.

Everything felt like a battle

I never signed up for

but still had to win.

Becoming Sunday

didn't happen overnight.

It happened in fragments—

one boundary at a time,

one healed wound at a time,

one truth spoken

after years of silence.

Becoming Sunday

was a rebirth—

not into someone new,

but into who I always was

before the world

told me to shrink.

She is softer now,

but not breakable.

She is wiser now,

but not hard.

She is whole now,

but not finished.

Becoming Sunday

means walking in purpose,

moving with intention,

loving with discernment,

and rising with clarity.

It means honoring the girl I was,

the woman I am,

and the legacy I'm building.

It means becoming

exactly who God always knew

I would grow into.

And baby—

I finally recognize her.

POEM 39 : THIS IS FOR MY EARTHS

(daughters, God daughters, nieces, cousins, and any earth in my space.)

This is for my daughters (earths)—

the ones born from my body,

that didn't make it but are still

In my spirit,

In my example.

For the earths watching me rise,

learning strength

from how I stand,

learning softness

from how I heal,

learning truth

from how I walk away

from what no longer honors me.

This is for the daughters

who don't yet know

how powerful they are

but carry destiny

in their bones.

I want you to know this:

Your voice matters.

Your dreams matter.

Your boundaries matter.

Your heart is worth protecting

without apology.

May you never shrink

to fit someone else's comfort.

May you never confuse struggle

with loyalty.

May you never lose yourself

trying to be loved.

And if the world ever tries

to dim your light—

shine harder.

You come from a lineage

of women who survived fire

and still learned how to glow.

You are not just my daughters—

you are my legacy.

POEM 40 : THIS IS FOR MY SUNS

(sons, God sons, nephews, cousins, and any suns in my space).

This is for my sons (suns)—

The ones who came from my body,

 but didn't make it

the ones who carry my lessons

in their walk,

in their heart,

in their becoming.

For the boys growing into men

in a world that tells them

not to feel,

not to break,

not to soften.

Let me tell you the truth:

Your emotions are not weakness.

Your vulnerability is not shame.

Your compassion is not a flaw.

You can be strong

and still be gentle.

You can be firm

and still be kind.

You can be powerful

and still protect the hearts

of the women around you.

I want you to know:

It is okay to cry.

It is okay to rest.

It is okay to ask for help.

It is okay to choose peace

over pride.

You are not just sons—

you are future leaders,

future fathers,

future healers,

future kings

who don't need a crown

to prove their worth.

And if you ever forget your value—

look at the strength you came from,

look at the love you were raised with,

look at the legacy you walk inside of.

You are my suns—

You are Suns of goddesses

and that alone

is greatness.

PART IV-

LEGACY, HEALING AND REBIRTH

POEM 41 : MAMA TAUGHT ME HOW TO LOVE

My mama didn't teach me love

through perfect moments

or fairy-tale endings—

she taught me through survival.

She taught me

that love is showing up

even when your heart is tired.

That love is holding on

even when the world

lets go of you.

She taught me

that love is flawed,

messy,

complicated,

and still worth fighting for.

She taught me

that you can be breaking

and still be a blessing,

that you can be hurting

and still give your best,

that you can lose everything

and still choose hope.

My mama taught me

that love is not loud—

it's consistent.

It's not perfect—

it's present.

It's not fantasy—

it's faith.

And even when she couldn't stay,

even when life pulled her away from me

before I understood why—

her love lingered.

In the way I forgive.

In the way I nurture.

In the way I rise

after every fall.

Mama taught me how to love—

not by being flawless,

but by being real.

And her real

was enough to shape me.

POEM 42 : MY GRANDMOTHERS ALTER

At my grandmother's altar,

I learned reverence.

Not the kind taught in church pews,

but the kind whispered

through the hands of women

who lived hard

and prayed harder.

She didn't speak God's name

in thunder—

she spoke it in chores,

in cooking pots,

in the gentle hum

of early-morning devotion.

Her altar wasn't carved

from fancy wood—

it was built from faith,

from discipline,

from the quiet strength

of a woman who carried

generations on her back.

When she prayed,

I swear the walls listened.

I swear the air stilled.

I swear the ancestors leaned in closer

to hear her heart.

She taught me

that holiness lives in habits—

in showing up,

in staying kind,

in forgiving faster

than the world wounds you.

Now,

when I kneel at my own altar,

I feel her.

In the way my voice softens.

In the way my spirit steadies.

In the way my prayers rise—

faithful, steady,

like her.

This altar is hers.

This altar is mine.

This altar is us.

A lineage of strength

that refuses to die.

POEM 43 : LEGACY AIN'T JUST BLOOD

People think legacy

is something you pass down

only through DNA—

but legacy ain't just blood.

Legacy is the people you teach,

the ones you lift,

the lives you soften,

the hearts you sharpen.

Legacy is the story you rewrite

so your children

don't have to survive it.

Legacy is choosing healing

over habit.

Peace

over pride.

Boundaries

over brokenness.

Legacy is every hand you held

until its shaking stopped.

Legacy is every child you raised

with your presence

even if you didn't birth them.

Legacy is every woman

you taught to rise

by rising yourself.

Legacy is the love

that will outlive your body.

The lessons

that will outlive your name.

The healing

that will outlive the pain

that once defined you.

Legacy ain't just blood—

it's impact.

It's intention.

It's the echo you leave

in every soul

you touched on purpose.

POEM 44 : HEALING LOOKS GOOD ON ME

For years,

I wore my wounds

like weather—

unpredictable,

heavy,

loud.

But healing—

healing came quiet.

First in small shifts,

like breathing deeper

than I used to.

Then in bigger ways—

like walking away

from people I once thought

I needed to survive.

Healing softened my voice

but strengthened my boundaries.

Healing unclenched my jaw

but sharpened my discernment.

Healing quieted my fear

but amplified my faith.

And now,

when I look at myself—

my glow,

my peace,

my presence,

my refusal to shrink—

I see a woman

reborn.

Healing looks good on me.

Not because it made me perfect,

but because it made me real.

Whole.

Aligned.

Aware.

This version of me

fits in my skin

like she was always meant to live here.

Healing looks good on me—

and I'm not done.

POEM 45 : THE WOMEN WHO REFUSED TO QUIT

I almost quit—

more times than I can count.

Quit healing.

Quit loving.

Quit believing.

Quit trying

to rewrite a life

that kept breaking faster

than I could rebuild it.

But every time I sat down

in my defeat,

something rose in me—

something ancient,

something fierce,

something tied to the bones

of women before me

who refused to be buried

in their pain.

The woman I am today

exists because the girl I was

refused to quit.

Even when her knees buckled.

Even when her hands shook.

Even when her voice cracked

under the weight

of every unspoken prayer.

She kept going—

not because she was fearless,

but because she was faithful.

I honor her now.

I thank her now.

She carried me

to this moment.

I am the woman

who refused to quit—

and that alone

is victory.

POEM 46 : EVEN IF YOU BROKE ME I'M WHOLE

You broke me—

not in one blow,

but in pieces.

A crack here,

a silence there,

a promise snatched back

before my heart could blink.

But here's the part

you never expected:

I didn't stay broken.

I stitched myself together
with boundaries and truth.
I healed wounds
you never apologized for.
I relearned my worth
in the absence of your love
and the presence of God's.

You were a chapter—
I am the book.

You were a moment—
I am the meaning.

You were a wound—

I am the healing.

Even if you broke me,

I'm whole.

Not because of you—

but in spite of you.

Not because I forgot—

but because I forgave.

Not because I returned—

but because I rose.

And the woman I am now

is untouchable

by the man you were then.

POEM 47 : I DON'T HATGE YOU-
I HEALED YOU

There was a time

your name tasted like rust

in my mouth—

bitterness and memory

swirled together

into something

I didn't know how to swallow.

I resented your choices.

Your lies.

Your absence.

Your betrayal.

Your refusal to become the man

I begged you to be.

But here is my truth now:

I don't hate you—

I healed you.

I healed the part of me

that kept asking "why."

I healed the version of myself

that believed your love

measured my worth.

I healed the wound

you left open

long after you walked away.

Healing didn't make me love you again—

it made me release you.

I don't hate you.

I don't need to.

Hate is heavy,

and I travel light.

You are no longer my burden,

no longer my lesson,

no longer my prayer.

Healing freed me

from defining myself

by the damage you caused.

So no—

I don't hate you.

I healed you.

And then,

I healed me.

POEM 48 : WHAT MY SCARS TAUGHT ME

My scars taught me

more than my victories ever did.

They taught me

how to rebuild myself

from the inside out.

How to love the woman

in the mirror

even when she was trembling.

How to stand tall

on days when my spirit

felt folded in half.

My scars taught me

that healing is not linear,

not gentle,

not always pretty.

But it is honest.

And it is worth it.

They taught me

that every wound

has a wisdom,

every ache

has a lesson,

every loss

has a rebirth.

My scars taught me
how to walk away.
How to discern peace
from attachment.
How to choose myself
without apologizing
for the choosing.

Most of all,
my scars taught me
that I am not fragile—
I am fortified.

And every mark on my body,

every memory in my bones,

every tear I ever shed

has shaped me into a woman

who rises without hesitation

and loves without fear.

These scars

are my teachers.

And I'm grateful

for what they made me.

A LETTER:

To the Men Who Held Me Up,

Thank you.

Not the kind of thank you

that gets tossed around casually—

but the kind that comes

from a healed place,

a grateful place,

a place that remembers

exactly who showed up

when life got too heavy.

You held me up

when my knees buckled.

You stood guard

when the world got loud.

You saw the woman in me

when I couldn't see her myself.

You didn't ask me to shrink.

You didn't fear my strength.

You didn't run

from my wounds.

You listened

when my spirit was shaking.

You covered me

without caging me.

You protected me

without silencing me.

Some of you were friends,

some family,

some brothers by soul,

some men sent by God

to remind me

what safety feels like.

You didn't fix me—

you steadied me.

You didn't rescue me—

you respected me.

You didn't define my healing—

you defended my peace

while I found it.

And to the men reading this—

whether you know it or not—

you made room

for the woman I am becoming.

This book carries your fingerprints

in the most honorable way.

Thank you

for presence.

Thank you

for protection.

Thank you

for choosing to be

the kind of men

who lift women higher

instead of weighing them down.

You will always be seen.

You will always be honored.

You will always be prayed for.

With deep respect and gratitude,

— Sunday Jones

POEM 49 : TO THE MEN WHO STAYED PROTECTED & HELD US DOWN

This is for the men

who stayed—

even when staying

meant weathering storms

they didn't create.

For the men who protect

without controlling,

who lead

without overpowering,

who hold space

without making it about them.

For the men

whose presence feels like safety,

whose voice softens madness,

whose arms reintroduce peace

to women who forgot

what peace felt like.

This is for the men

who don't run

when our trauma shows up—

who sit with us

in the unraveling

and help us weave ourselves

back whole.

For the men

who watch our healing

with reverence,

who water our growth,

who speak life into us

when the world tries

to drain us dry.

We honor you.

We see you.

We cherish you.

We pray for you.

May your steps be ordered.

May your purpose be protected.

May your light never dim.

May your hearts never harden.

To the men who stayed,

protected,

and held us down—

this poem

is your gratitude.

REFLECTION PROMPT

What Did This Book Awaken in You?

Take a breath.

Take your time.

Take inventory of your heart.

What rose to the surface as you moved through
these pages?

What memories did you meet again,
and what truths did you finally release?

What part of you felt seen?

What part of you felt challenged?

What part of you felt healed?

Let these questions guide you:

- What pain have you outgrown?

- What love do you now deserve?

- What boundaries feel sacred now?

- What version of you is emerging?

- What are you finally ready to forgive?

Write it.

Speak it.

Claim it.

Because reflection

is the bridge

between who you were

and who you are becoming.

This book wasn't written

to just be read—it was written

to awaken.

What awakened in you?

"BONUS SECTION"

LETTER TO MY YOUNGER SELF

Dear Younger Me,

I wish I could reach back through time
and hold your face in my hands,
look you in your wide, trembling eyes
and tell you the truth:

None of what they did
was your fault.

You were just a child—
soft-hearted, wide-open,
trusting people
who should've protected you
but didn't know how.

I'm sorry you had to grow up

before your spirit was ready.

Sorry you had to swallow secrets

bigger than your small shoulders.

Sorry you had to be strong

before you ever felt safe.

But hear me now:

You did not break.

You adapted.

You survived.

You learned how to breathe

beneath weight

that was never meant

for your little lungs.

I want you to know

that the world will try to dim you,

but you will shine anyway.

Life will try to harden you,

but you will soften again.

People will underestimate you,

but you will rise beyond

every limitation they placed on your name.

You will grow into a woman

who walks with God,

with clarity,

with boundaries,

with purpose that pours from her chest

like light.

And all the parts of you

that felt forgotten—

I carried them.

I nurtured them.

I turned them into wisdom.

Thank you

for surviving what you never deserved.

Thank you

for keeping the pieces

even when you didn't know

what they would become.

I honor you.

I love you.

I promise to protect you

from here on out.

With the gentleness you were owed,

— Your Future Self (Sunday)

POEM 50: "LITTLE GIRL I FOUND YOU"

Little girl,

I found you—

curled in the corners of silence,

hiding your hurt

behind bravery too big

for a body so small.

I saw the fear in your eyes

masked as obedience.

Saw the loneliness

you wrapped in make-believe.

Saw the dreams you tucked

beneath your pillow

hoping no one would steal them.

I found you

in every woman I became—

in the tiny flinch

when kindness felt unfamiliar,

in the way you apologized

just for existing,

in the way you walked through life

expecting danger

even in safe rooms.

But hear me now, baby girl—

I am here.

I am the woman

you prayed for.

I am the protector

you needed.

I am the voice

you didn't have.

Come out of hiding.

Let your small hands rest.

You don't have to fight anymore.

You don't have to guess

who will hurt you.

You don't have to pretend

you're strong

when you're breaking.

Little girl,

I found you—

and I'm not leaving.

I brought softness with me,

and safety,

and truth.

I brought a new name,

new strength,

new purpose.

I came to tell you:

You make it.

You heal.

You rise.

You become.

And the woman I am today

is the proof.

LETTER TO MY FUTURE SELF

Dear Future Me,

I'm writing to you with the awareness
that everything I'm healing now
is clearing the path you will walk on.

I hope when you read this
you are standing somewhere
that once felt impossible.
I hope your shoulders are softer,
your heart is fuller,
your spirit is steadier.

I hope you're surrounded
by people who honor your boundaries,

match your effort,

protect your peace,

and celebrate your becoming.

If life is good when you read this—

breathe it in.

You earned that softness.

You fought for that rest.

You prayed for that clarity.

Don't rush through your blessings

like you're still living in survival mode.

And if life is heavy when you read this—

remember:

You've made it through worse.

You've risen from what tried to bury you.

You have never been abandoned by God.

You are never alone.

Dear Future Me,

I want you to keep choosing joy

without justification,

love without losing yourself,

purpose without apology.

Keep your voice open.

Keep your heart discerning.

Keep your spirit alert.

And most of all—

never forget the girl you were,

the woman you became,

and the force you are stepping into.

I'm proud of you already.

With hope and honor,

— Your Present Self (Sunday)

POEM 51: "One Day, You'll Thank Me"

One day,

you'll thank me—

not for being perfect,

but for being persistent.

For showing up

on days my body was tired

and my spirit was trembling.

For choosing healing

when hurt felt easier.

For choosing growth

when comfort felt safer.

For choosing truth

when silence felt smoother.

One day,

you'll look back

at the woman I am now—

the one doing the heavy lifting,

the emotional labor,

the unlearning,

the forgiving,

the rebuilding—

and you'll whisper:

"Thank you, for not giving up on me."

Because every boundary I set,

every tear I released,

every prayer I whispered,

every wound I closed—

I did it

for us.

I did it so you could love freely,

so you could rest deeply,

so you could rise fully,

so you could walk in rooms

with a confidence

that was once just a seed.

One day,

you'll stand taller

because I kneeled.

You'll move lighter

because I let go.

You'll breathe easier

because I healed.

And when that day comes,

when you meet the future

I'm building piece by piece—

I hope you smile,

place your hand over your heart,

and say:

"She made me possible."

POEM 52 : "Letter to My Healing"

Dear Healing,

You came slow—

like sunrise through thick clouds,

like a whisper trying to make itself known

in a room full of noise.

I didn't recognize you at first.

You didn't look like peace.

You didn't feel like comfort.

You didn't arrive soft.

You came as endings

I didn't want,

truths I wasn't ready for,

boundaries I had to build

with trembling hands.

You came as loneliness

that taught me self-worth,

silence that taught me self-trust,

and clarity

that taught me self-love.

Dear Healing,

you were not pretty—

but you were necessary.

You stripped me,

then rebuilt me.

You broke me open,

then filled me with light.

You brought me truth

I didn't want,

and peace

I didn't think I deserved.

And now—

I thank you.

For making me softer

without making me weak.

For making me wiser

without making me cold.

For making me whole

without hiding my scars.

Dear Healing,

you saved my life

one revelation at a time.

And I will honor you

by never going back

to the woman

who didn't know her worth.

POEM 53 : "Dear Future Love"

Dear Future Love,

I hope you arrive gently—

not because I am fragile,

but because I grew up in storms.

I hope your presence feels like calm,

like exhaling after years

of bracing for impact.

I'm not asking you to fix me—

the healing was my job.

But I do ask one thing:

come with truth.

Come with consistency.

Come with intention.

I am no longer a woman

who entertains half-love,

almost-love,

dangerous love,

or love that must be survived.

I am ready for a love

that feels like alignment—

not confusion.

A love that feels like peace—

not recovery.

A love that feels like home—

not a battlefield.

Future love,

when you show up—

I will be ready.

Ready with boundaries,

with softness,

with discernment,

with a heart that knows how to give

without losing itself again.

And I pray

you are a man who recognizes

that my softness

was won in war,

and treats it

like the treasure it is.

Until then—

I am becoming the woman

you will be grateful to love.

REFLECTION: WHAT ARE YOU BECOMING ?

Take a moment with yourself.

Settle your breath.

Settle your heart.

Settle your truth.

Use this page to sit with the version of you

that finished this book—

the version who is softer, clearer, wiser,

and more aligned than she was

when she first opened these pages.

Consider reflecting on:

- What part of my story did this book touch?

- What truth did I face that I've been avoiding?

- What wound am I finally ready to release?

- What version of myself am I stepping into?

- What do I want to forgive?

- What do I want to protect?

- What am I ready to claim?

- What will I no longer apologize for?

- What does healing look like for me now?

Write freely.

Write honestly.

Write without judgment.

You are the author of your next chapter.

AUTHOR'S NOTE

This book was not written from a place of perfection—

it was written from a place of becoming.

Every poem, every letter, every reflection inside these pages

comes from truth I had to face, pain I had to release,

and healing I had to choose—over and over again.

I did not write this book to reopen wounds.

I wrote it to show what it looks like

to survive them, learn from them,

and eventually rise because of them.

Some parts of this story were hard to revisit.

Some chapters took longer to write

because the girl I used to be

was still waiting to be heard.

But I wrote them anyway.

Not for sympathy.

Not for shock.

Not for applause.

I wrote them so that someone—maybe you—

could feel seen in their own struggle

and be reminded that brokenness is not the end.

Healing is possible.

Peace is possible.

Becoming is possible.

My only intention with this work

is to honor my truth

and give you permission to honor yours.

If something in these pages touched you,

challenged you,

freed you,

or even simply held your hand for a moment—

then this book has done what it was born to do.

Thank you for reading with an open heart.

Thank you for walking through these scars with me.

And thank you for allowing me to speak

the gospel according to my pain.

With love and truth,

— Sunday Jones

ABOUT THE AUTHOR

Sunday Jones writes from the trenches and the triumph. A storyteller at heart, she weaves healing, wisdom, and truth into every line—blending poetry, testimony, and spiritual reflection with raw honesty and emotional power. Her work is rooted in survival and shaped by resilience. Through her writing, performances, radio segments, and community work, she offers a voice to those who have lived through pain and are still rising from it.

Sunday is the founder of Sunday Jones Enterprises and the creative force behind Sunday Jones Productions. She continues to build safe spaces, inspire transformation, and walk boldly in her divine becoming.

www.sundayjoneswrites.com

Closing Blessing for Your Journey

May every truth you met in these pages
set you free.

May every wound that was reopened
be finally released.

May every tear you shed
water the life
you are about to walk into.

May your heart trust again,
but with wisdom.

May your spirit soften again,
but with boundaries.

May your feet move toward purpose,

not pain.

May the ancestors guide you,

God cover you,

clarity lead you,

and peace protect you.

May you never shrink again.

May you never settle again.

May you never forget your worth again.

And above all—

may you rise

with a quiet power

that cannot be taken,

shaken,

or silenced.

You are becoming.

You are worthy.

You are whole.

Walk in it.

— Blessings & Love,

Sunday Jones

IF SCARS COULD SPEAK:

THE GOSPEL ACCORDING TO MY PAIN

by Sunday Jones

254 PGS